IMAGES C   ᒐᗩᑎᗪ

Cudworth
& Grimethorpe

Cudworth schoolgirls at the Welfare Park bandstand, *c.* 1930. The man standing in the centre is thought to be local schoolmaster Mr. Jones. This picture, which can also be seen on the cover, captures the fashions of the late 1920s, the bell-shaped cloche hats and white knee-length socks.

Making a splash at Cudworth's open-air swimming pool, *c.* 1950. In these days there were no rules outlawing the time honoured practices of 'bombing', 'somersaults', 'ducking' or 'dunking'. Flowery bathing-caps and one piece costumes were *de rigeur* for the girls; boys would attempt to impress with bigger and better splashes.

IMAGES OF ENGLAND

Cudworth & Grimethorpe

Matthew Young

NONSUCH

Cudworth St. John's church and Methodist chapel peformance of *Aladdin* in 1949.

First published 1996
This new pocket edition 2006
Images unchanged from first edition

Nonsuch Publishing Limited
The Mill, Brimscombe Port,
Stroud, Gloucestershire, GL5 2QG
www.nonsuch-publishing.com

Nonsuch Publishing is an imprint of Tempus Publishing Group

© Matthew Young, 1996

The right of Matthew Young to be identified as the Author
of this work has been asserted in accordance with the
Copyrights, Designs and Patents Act 1988.

All rights reserved. No part of this book may be reprinted
or reproduced or utilised in any form or by any electronic,
mechanical or other means, now known or hereafter invented,
including photocopying and recording, or in any information
storage or retrieval system, without the permission in writing
from the Publishers.

British Library Cataloguing in Publication Data.
A catalogue record for this book is available from the British Library.

ISBN 1-84588-267-9

Typesetting and origination by Nonsuch Publishing Limited
Printed in Great Britain by Oaklands Book Services Limited

Contents

Acknowledgements

Gillian Nixon and Louise Whitworth at Barnsley Archive Service for their help and advice; Fiona Lewis who introduced me to numerous people in Cudworth; Dave Shaw for all his information and guidance; Constance Shaw for allowing me to use some of her precious family pictures; the members of the Village Club and the other friendly clubs and societies in the area; Geoff Govier for kind permission to reproduce some of his Shafton pictures; Pat Owers, who not only ran against Dorothy Hyman and supplied me with numerous athletics facts and figures but also gave birth to a gorgeous daughter (though not all simultaneously).

Mistakes or factual errors are entirely the fault of the author but he would appreciate and welcome any further information (or critical assessment) concerning the pictures presented here.

'I can see Brierley now the pit has gone'
(A local saying sung to the tune of *I can see clearly now* – Johnny Nash 1971).

Introduction

'But I *love* Cudworth. I've been to many posh cities as an athlete – New York, Tokyo, Rome, Moscow, Perth, Stockholm – but I wouldn't like to live in any of them, in fact I wouldn't like to live in a city at all. Fancy hardly knowing your next-door-neighbour! International athletics has taken me far away from our village and enabled me to travel the world, but beneath it all I am a home bird. Now I'm content to live in Cudworth all the rest of my life'. (Dorothy Hyman, *Sprint to Fame*, 1964. London, Sydney Paul). Dorothy Hyman's words may have been written over forty years ago but the sentiments remain true today. Cudworth and the surrounding villages of Grimethorpe, Shafton and Brierley still have that strong sense of identity and, most importantly, community – something which has seeped away in many of the towns and cities of this country. Open the doors to any of the pubs and clubs in the area and the room is thick with first names and friendly banter. The information for many of these photographs has come from local people: they supplied the names to the faces. I must thank everyone who allowed me to impose so freely upon their time. Local history books mean very little if they are simply a long procession of photographs; it is the information behind the pictures which brings them to life and allows the sparks of memory to ignite.

The name Cudworth is probably derived from 'Cutha' – an early Nordic settler and the area he would have called home would have been his 'worth'. Grimethorpe is also derived from Nordic origins: 'Grimr' is a Norse god and 'thorpe' being a village or hamlet. Records are unclear which Saxon nobles held the lands around Grimethorpe or Cudworth but after the Norman Conquest of 1066 the area would have been carved up by the faithful retinue of William I. Land was the currency of the day in medieval times and England, a newly conquered territory, was divided up between the earls, lords and knights of Normandy. Brierley (then spelt Brereley) and the surrounding lands which would have included Cudworth and Grimethorpe became a feudal fief of Ilbert de Laci who in turn may have divided his lands amongst others on the observance of homage and fealty. During the twelfth century one of Ilbert's sons, Adam Fitz Swein, gave gifts of land to the monks of St John at Pontefract, this would have included areas around Carlton and Brierley. These gifts provided the means for the establishment of the Monk Bretton priory in 1154. The priory would have acted as a focus for the local population; medieval cottage industries would supply the needs of the monks while tenant farmers would supply the priory with a fee or tithe in the form of part of the local harvest. After the Dissolution the lands around Cudworth and Grimethorpe passed through the hands of several noble families: Bolles, Jobson, Herrington, Stanley, Dymond. The land was essentially rural and would remain so until the latter part of the last century. In 1379 a census stated that Cudworth contained ninety-eight persons over the age of sixteen and this had risen to only 1,607 by 1891. The lands around the villages were renowned for sweeping parkland and the variety of trees. This rural idyll was under threat when the railways came to Cudworth after the 1840s and would vanish after the pits were sunk at the turn of the century. The crushing forces of industrialisation and urbanisation would yet again take precedent.

Cudworth was chosen as the site on the main line north from which to service Barnsley. The line opened on 30 June 1840 and brought the first influx of new workers to the area. The impractical nature of situating the Barnsley station so far outside the town was overcome in May 1870 with the completion of the 'push and pull' extension into Barnsley; a later line linking Cudworth and Wombwell opened in September 1899.

Although the railways established the communication links to the rest of the country it was the sinking of the pits that brought employment and forged the contemporary communities. The coal seams of South Yorkshire dip gradually from west to east. The early shafts dug around Silkstone and west of Barnsley were only a few feet deep and rapidly exhausted; at Grimethorpe the first seam is at a depth of 586 yards sloping away to 924 yards at Thorne. From 1870 onward the pits began to open around the area: Monk Bretton (1870), Carlton (1879), Grimethorpe (1897), Frickley (1905), Ferrymoor (1917). Consequently the population rose dramatically: the census records Cudworth's growth from 1,607 in 1891, 6,824 in 1911 to 9,377 in 1931. Grimethorpe grew from a small hamlet of a few hundred at the turn of the century to a large village with a population of 2,906 in 1921. This new and growing population required housing, shops, civic amenities, pubs, schools, religious instruction – the building blocks of a settled community. King Coal may have fuelled the Industrial Revolution but it also made the villages of Cudworth, Grimethorpe, Shafton and Brierley.

The pictures within this book chart the one hundred years since the sinking of the pits. Each photograph is a snapshot in time and rewarding to the receptive eye: the bustle of Barnsley Road and Goldthorpe High Street; street celebrations for coronations and jubilees; football teams in knee-length shorts. These old scenes have been collected over a number of years by the Barnsley Archive Service; the Service does important work in preserving the area's past and anyone with time to spare will enjoy a browse through the documents and pictures. My thanks must go to the staff at the Central Library for allowing access to such images. The pace of life presented here may have gone forever but these pictures provide a thread to the past and form a part of our heritage.

One

At the Heart of Cudworth

The Crescent, *c.* 1920, a peaceful and idyllic scene taken just after the construction of the Village Club (right) and the removal of the old boundary walls. McAdoo's (centre) has taken over the premises that had previously belonged to Blakeley's drapery and millinery shop.

The Crescent, *c.* 1912. The old walls (and the trees) which surrounded the Crescent were removed soon after this photograph was taken. The shops on the Crescent at this time were, left to right: The Globe Tea Company; X.L. Company shaving saloon and tobacconist; Blakeley drapery and milliner; Holling's clothing; Eastmans Limited; the hardware store.

A procession through The Crescent just before the First World War. This parade may well be a Whitsuntide Walk although the decorative floats and banners suggest a more formal gathering.

A view across The Pond toward the edge of The Crescent and the start of the Barnsley Road, c. 1950. The Victoria Hotel stands next to the Globe Tea Company Shop which is now the site of Anchor Press printing company.

Further along The Crescent, c. 1950. Bramham's grocery store stands next to David Haigh Limited, an emporium for clothing, bedding, hats and furniture. Today the shops on the Crescent are: Anchor Press, Spot on Taxis, Crescent News. The other sites remain empty.

A very old and rare view up Barnsley Road to The Crescent, c. 1890. The old library stands to the left and the entrance to Syndale Road and the school (now G & G Doubleglazing) can be seen on the right. At the top of picture is the site of the barn and farmhouse which stood before the first Village Club was constructed.

A view over the Pond, *c.* 1930. At one time there was a pond situated here which in winter was the site of some enthusiastic amateur skating; although there is little surface water here today the name has remained. The old Village Club was demolished in the 1970s (to some local consternation) and a replacement built further down the hill.

The same view over Pond Corner taken over twenty five years later. The changes that have been made are few: a public phone box, bus shelter and street lighting are the only new additions. Sadly the Market Cross is one of the monuments missing from the pond today.

Two

Along the Barnsley Road

The entrance to Cudworth essentially begins at the railway bridge. The original bridge, rumours persist, was built without enough passing room for high-sided vehicles: one story tells of a Barnsley-bound bus stuck fast beneath the bridge with several puzzled officials looking on. The problem was solved by a passing Cudworth man who told them to let down the tyres allowing the bus to move forward. The story is almost certainly apocryphal but soon after the construction of the bridge the road beneath was lowered to allow for 'taller' traffic.

The bottom of the Barnsley Road, *c.* 1910. Many of the cottages along the main road had just been constructed to cope with the influx of new workers to the area. They tended to be built on a piecemeal basis according to the funds of independent developers. The houses built at this time include: Highfield Place (1893), The Knoll (1892), Bock Villas (1897), Rock Cottages (1905), The Bays (1910).

A view up the Barnsley Road taken almost from the same position as the previous picture but almost forty years later. There seems little difference in the condition of the housing but the road surface has been tarmaced and drains put in.

Right: The Barnsley Road in 1970 – the only new addition to the road appears to be overhanging street lighting.

Below: The Barnsley Road, c. 1930 looking toward the junction with St John's Road and Prospect Street. On the right, behind the two boys, was Cudworth's first cinema or picture palace which was demolished after the opening of the 'Rock' at the Pond; presently the site is owned by Robert's furniture store.

BARNSLEY ROAD. CUDWORTH. — 7.

Barnsley Road, Cudworth.

Barnsley Road at the corner with Prospect, *c.* 1958. The shop on the this corner was a pawn brokers before it belonged to Harrah's stores. Over the road stood Horton's electrical shop, Fenton's, Robert's, Brady Webster's grocers. The wooden frame of the old bus stop is just visible on the extreme left.

Left: A later view of Barnsley Road and Prospect, *c.* 1970. The traffic through the town has increased over the years and congestion along the Barnsley Road is a regular sight. At the time of writing the long awaited bypass is due to be constructed behind the park – whether this provides a relief for the centre of the town remains to be seen.

Below: Looking down the Barnsley Road in 1935 at the corner of St John's Street and Prospect Street (left) and Bank Street (right).

Barnsley Road, c. 1935. The shops on the left of the main road have changed hands over the years. Today they are (from the bottom of Barnsley Road): Lukis chip shop, Foster's bakers, Travelink, Geo's bookie, C. & A. Booth's florist, Ian Walker's solicitors, Robert's furniture, The Halifax, Guys and Girls, The Freezer Centre.

Barnsley Road at the turn of the twentieth century; standing for any length of time on the edge of the main road today will probably result in a rapid visit to the Accident and Emergency Department. The situation at this point has been somewhat eased by the installation of the pedestrian crossing but one hundred years ago it was possible to cross over without risking limbs or an assault upon the respiratory system. On the right of the road the shops occupying the sites are today Dewhirst butchers and Special Occasions; the building under construction is Ian and Jackie's fruit and vegetable shop; the tea shop is now a pharmacy.

Barnsley Road looking toward the John Smith Methodist chapel, *c.* 1920.

A similar view looking toward the Methodist chapel taken in 1925.

A rare picture, taken in 1905, of the chapel. The Gladstone cottages on the right are amongst the oldest in the town being built in 1895.

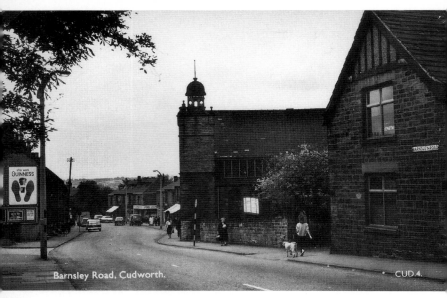

Barnsley Road, Cudworth.

CUD.4.

A view down the Barnsley Road taken in the 1960s showing the chapel and the council offices and library.

Three

Along the Pontefract Road

Pontefract Road, c. 1935.

Pontefract Road, *c.* 1930. The sweet shop (which is now a take-away) on the right later became a chemist's and would at one time belong to Walt Walker the undertaker.

Looking down the Pontefract Road *c.* 1930. J.H. Holmes is on the extreme right, a site today occupied by King D.I.Y. The Cudworth (far right) has yet to be built.

The Manse on the Pontefract Road, c. 1905. In the background is the Cudworth 39th Branch of the Barnsley Co-operative Society.

A more recent view of The Manse in 1970. Apart from the obvious increase in traffic little has changed.

The Albert Club on Albert Street, *c.* 1930.

Four

The Welfare Park

The Lily Pond at the Miners' Welfare Park, c. 1960.

Rose and flower beds were planted to provide a picturesque setting for local people to relax.

MINERS WELFARE PARK. CUDWORTH. 15.

A view across the Welfare Park to the greenhouse, c. 1950.

Inside the greenhouse at the Welfare Park, c. 1950. The gentleman pictured here is possibly Mr Warmsley who was the park keeper for many years. All manner of exotic plants were grown inside the glass walls, including banana trees. During the summer the greenhouse was opened to the public to inspect all the interesting flora and fauna.

The paddling pool at the Welfare Park soon after opening c. 1930s. The thick pullovers and jackets of the children suggest that it is probably not the weather to brave a paddle. During the coldest winters the pool became a makeshift ice ring which was free to all those with or without skates.

The paddling pool in warmer weather, *c.* 1940. The small boy wading his way through the pool is thought to be Harry Rodbourne.

Paddling Pool, Cudworth Park.

CUD.3.

To the side of the paddling pool were three tennis courts built as part of the expansion of the park. The courts, which were concrete, became difficult to maintain; they were dug up and the site seeded for use as a bowling green. As this scene from the 1960s shows the area to the side has yet to be developed but would later become a 'pitch and putt' for adventurous golfers. Putters and wedges could be obtained from a wooden hut near the paddling pool; bunkers were erected near to the top of the park.

Creating a splash at the paddling pool c. 1970. The pool was filled in during 1994, landscaped and made into a play area. The Cudworth Public Conveniences were also located at the edge of the park but were later moved to the Barnsley Road.

The open-air swimming pool at Cudworth was always popular in the summer. The original pool was dug in the 1930s complete with fountains and individual changing huts. An indoor pool was constructed on the site in the 1960s but the due to foundation problems it was demolished; the area is now Rose Terrace flats and bungalows.

A view of the bandstand soon after opening in the 1930s. For many local people Sunday afternoons were always spent around the stand watching a local brass band play while the children played in the park or in the paddling pool. Such luminaries as the Grimethorpe Colliery band were regular features. The drift of musical notes could heard in Shafton and Grimethorpe and would announce an afternoon of relaxation before the start of another working week. For a younger generation the 'park shed' was notorious as a meeting place for courting couples.

The Bandstand, Cudworth.

A later view of the bandstand in the Welfare Park c. 1950. The trees have now grown to maturity and the stand itself has been lowered for ease of access. Later the stand would be taken away leaving only memories to drift across the park.

Five

Around and About

Ring Farm on Carrs Lane, *c.* 1900. The two elegantly dressed ladies are standing on the wooden footbridge which crosses Small Bridge Dike. Much of the land in Low Cudworth (including Ring Farm) was owned by the Silverwood family. The farm is now owned by South Yorkshire Mounted Police as the training site and stables for all their horses.

Two views down Lunn Road at the junction with Manor Road showing the old well (far right) which was, somewhat inconveniently, near the middle of the road.

Lazenby's farm in Low Cudworth, *c.* 1910.

A later view of Lazenby's farm, possibly 1960. On the left is the old beer-off.

Low Cudworth *c.* 1960. On the hillside it is possible to see the Crown Estates and the houses along the Darfield Road as Cudworth's post-war development stretched eastwards.

A view over Low Cudworth in 1970 looking toward Sunny Bank.

Looking down Lunn Road at the junction with St John's Road in 1904.

A very old and rare photograph of School Hill at the junction with the Snydale Road, Barnsley Road and Market Street, c. 1895.

Crosby Croft cottages on the Royston Road, *c.* 1925. These houses, just outside Shafton, were owned by the National Coal Board and leased to officials and managers working at nearby collieries. Some locals refer to this part of the Royston Road as 'Toffs Lane'.

TOWN STREET, SHAFTON.

Town Street, Shafton, *c.* 1915; the street is today called High Street.

Many old mile stones can be seen around Cudworth and Grimethorpe, especially near the ancient tracks and paths that criss-cross the open fields between the villages. This particular marker, announcing the distance to Penistone, is found in the fields behind the Welfare Park and close to the edge of the Carlton Nature Reserve.

One of the new homes built on the Newlands estate in the 1960s as a temporary solution to the housing problem in the area. Unfortunately, temporary became a flexible term and these homes have required bracing and regular maintenance to keep them as viable housing stock. The rebuilding of the Crown Estates on the Darfield Road has shown the way forward, but the key to such projects is finance and community will. The principal housing estates built by the Council before the war were Newtown, Sidcop, Albert, Snydale, Darfield. These comprised a total of 650 pre-war homes; further developments after the war brought this total to 1,550.

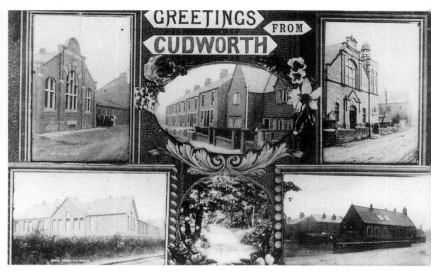

Every town in the country seems to have a composite view card and Cudworth is no exception. These two examples, from the early 1920s, show a carefully selected group of vignettes with the hope of catching the attention of the recipient. One card however has included a view of Church Street in Royston; surely Cudworth had a large enough range of views, buildings and subject matter to make a complete card?!

Six

Around Grimethorpe and Brierley

A charming view of Brierley village looking down Church Street in 1906. The Church of St. Paul was built in 1869 by John Wade from the contributions of George Savile-Foljambe.

Brierley Church and the Board School on Church Street, *c.* 1905.

Brierley Manor House, *c.* 1970. The house is actually closer to Grimethorpe than Brierley and can only be reached by track extending from Burntwood Road. The farm house is essentially eighteenth and nineteenth-century but retains fragments of the late medieval period at the rear of the building. It is a listed house under the protection of the Department of Environment. In their excellent history of Brierley M.R. Watson and M. Harrison have noted that following the succession of the Saville family to the Manor in 1617 large sums were spent on renovating the house (M. Harrison and M.R. Watson, *Brereley. A History of Brierley*). (1975). For many centuries the Manor of Brierley (Brereley) was one of the most important in Yorkshire and extended south through what is today Grimethorpe. In the seventeenth century the Lord of the Manor (Lord Talbot) extended his parkland and the village of Grimethorpe almost vanished from the map. Only after the sinking of the pits and the arrival of the railways did Grimethorpe's population begin to increase beyond that of Brierley.

Lindley House, Brierley is situated at the end of Church Street and the junction with Common Road (known locally as Cordeaux Corner). In the 1840 this house belonged to the Hoyland family and was actually called Brierley Hall. The site of the present Brierley Hall was at this stage farmland; this land was purchased by the Rev. John Hoyland and the the present Hall was built.

The old Brierley Post Office, c. 1976.

High Street, Grimethorpe, *c.* 1910.

H. Gledhall's grocery store at Grimethorpe, *c.* 1910.

The Colliery Offices at Grimthorpe, *c.* 1910.

A picture up Ladywood Road taken from Burntwood Road, *c.* 1925. The children in this photograph have obviously been told by the photographer to stand very still !

A horse and cart proceeds up Park Road not long after these houses were built in around 1910.

In the High Street at Grimethorpe, c. 1925.

Church Street, Grimethorpe, c. 1910.

Brierley Village, c. 1906.

Grimethorpe Hall in 1980. In December 1669 Robert Seaton married Theodicia Adwick of Ardsey and as a token of love (and as a family home) Robert built Grimethorpe. The building has been drastically altered over the years, receiving renovations in every following century.

Fold Head Farm, Grimethorpe in 1975. This farm (and the following building) are amongst the oldest in the area and were photographed as part of European heritage project.

Above: Bridge Farm near Grimethorpe in 1975.

Right: Flat caps and cloche hats are plentiful in this 1920s scene at the Grimethorpe War Memorial.

Inside St. Luke's church at Grimethorpe, *c.* 1910. The rapid growth in Grimethorpe's population brought the necessity of religious instruction. At the turn of the century those followers of the Church of England had to receive instruction at a temporary hut; however due to work of the first vicar, Rev. W.A. Holiday, sufficient funds were donated to enable construction to begin on St. Luke's church. The Lord of the Manor, the Hon. F.J.S. Foljambe donated the site and funded the construction of the vicarage and, on the 1 November 1902, Lady Gertrude Foljambe performed the laying of the foundation stone for which she was awarded an ornate silver trowel.

Brierley Hall in 1975 – a European heritage photograph. When Brierley village became part of Hemwsworth Rural District the hall was used as the headquarters for the Rural District Council.

Two views at sunset over Grimethorpe in the weeks before the colliery finally closed. The pit head, chimneys and cooling towers have now gone as the area comes to terms with a new economic era.

The changing skyline – Grimethorpe at sunset in the late 1980s.

Seven

Days of Learning

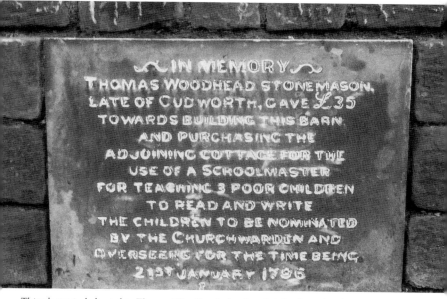

This plaque is dedicated to Thomas Woodhead who founded the first school in Cudworth in 1700s. Education was a 'hit and miss' affair of parental instruction and voluntary church schools for most children before the Forster Act of 1870. Most communities relied upon the generous nature of men such as Thomas Woodhead (and a William Poppleton who was to donate £50 – no small sum in Georgian England).

In 1870 Forster's Education Act was passed instituting state funded and maintained elementary schools; this was designed to fill gaps in the existing voluntary system by the creation of a local authority and school board. By the late Victorian period consensus had finally concluded that the working classes were no longer the 'swinish herd' but the future of a nation. The Reform Act of 1867 and the Forster Act were the start of a long (and painfully slow) period of necessary change. The realisation that the old order could no longer be sustained had become ingrained: change would take place through revolution or reform. As Robert Lowe's popular dictum of the day stated, 'We must educate our future masters', the seeds for twentieth century success would have to be sown early.

St John's National school (later called the Pond school) was built in 1851 and taught over 240 children. Under the provisions of the Forster Act existing voluntary schools could continue despite the creation of the public funded board schools. The school remained open until 1935 when Cudworth Modern school was built. The building was used for many years as a clothing factory but today is the premises of G & G double glazing.

The first board schools opened in Cudworth after the turn of the century. The West Riding Authority provided the funding for the Snydale Road and Pontefract Road schools. The Snydale opened the doors to pupils in 1901 at a cost of £6,000 and had over 400 pupils registered in its first year. Although the Forster Act took many years before the effects were felt it was a giant step towards creating a common level of education. Elementary education was made mandatory in 1880 but it was not until 1891 that it became entirely free. One of the clauses in the original Forster Act (Cowper-Temple clause) was ground-breaking: although religious instruction could be given in Board schools it could not be sectarian or of a single denomination.

Before the completion of the Snydale Road school this building, just off the Barnsley Road, served as a temporary classroom. It later became a Y.M.C.A. and many locals remember playing snooker here until late at night. It was demolished in the late 1970s.

Such was the rapid growth of population in Cudworth that new schools had to be provided. Birkwood Infants was built to cater for the families of the Crown Estates in the East of the town.

Two classes from the newly created Board school showing a plethora of petticoats, lace collars and hobnail boots. Note the long plank that has been provided for front row to sit upon.

Childen at play in the 'yard' at Snydale Road school, *c.* 1950.

Headstands and handstands at Snydale Road school in 1955. The essential requirement for a successful handstand was a 'trustworthy' friend to hold flailing legs; failure could result in the gymnast becoming a crumpled mass upon the floor. Note the tiny felt mats which were provided to 'cushion and support'.

A Snydale Road infant class of 1929. Top row, left to right: -?-, Gwen Sanderson, -?-, Betty Turnbull, -?-, Brian Blonfield, Betty Gregory, -?-, Greta Woofit, Tommy Walker. Second row: Doreen Chappel, Ken Holloway, Mary Hooper, Rene Williams, – ? -, Rene Fenn, Elsie Heals, Tom Clay, -?-. Third row: Connie Simons, George Wilmot, Gladys Crapper, -?-, Ella Bloomfield, Ken Hooper (last on the row). Fourth row: Gordon Race, Albert Sawage, Edna Barker, Betsy Lumm, -?-, Violet Kershaw, -?-, Joan Dewsnap. Front row: -?-, George Evans, -?-, Edna Hanks, -?- .

Above: A Snydale Road class in the late 1950s. Those identified include Susan Shaw, Hazel Jones, Janet Hamer.

Left: A Snydale school sports day and the Tug-of-War event *c.* 1950.

The children of Snydale Road school built a model of 'Cutha's Worth' which was on display in the 1950s.

The Secondary Modern school on Snydale Road was built in 1935 to provide education for the children of the area after an elementary grounding. The official opening took place on 25 May 1935 under the auspecies of Alderman W.E. Raley, OBE, vice-chairman of the Barnsley Education Committee. The school was built a cost of £18,000 and would accommodate 240 boys and 240 girls. The *Barnsley Chronicle* reported that 'the sunny aspect of the classrooms has been the most important consideration'. Today the site is a business park and most of Cudworth's young make the trip to Willowgarth at Grimethorpe.

Some of those who took part in the opening ceremony. Front row, left to right: Alderman T.H. Foulstone, Mr S. Lightowler (headmaster), Alderman W.E. Raley, F. Langmead, Mr W. M. Hyman, Mr G.A. Griffiths MP, Alderman J. Newton. The school was designed with all modern conveniences. In his short history of Cudworth H.W.M. Kirkby describes the new school: 'Cloakrooms are provided and the lavatories are fitted with hot and cold water. There is little playground but the extensive grounds are set out with trees, flower beds, lawns and a lily pond. The gymnasium is fitted with the latest equipment including shower baths'.

The bunting was out at the school in May 1937 for the Coronation celebrations and a special lunch was served at the dining room. The West Riding Education Authority also caught the celebratory mood: pupils were each given a special souvenir spoon to mark the occasion.

The boys of Cudworth Modern founded a fanciers' club in the grounds of the school. Animals that were kept included rabbits, hamsters, mice, pigeons and bees and pupils would even arrive early to help feed and clean their pets.

The club gained many prizes around the area, travelling as far as London to collect prizes. Every year a 'fur and feathers' show was held at the school to the amazement of locals and several competitions were held against a similar club from Ashford in Kent.

Printed on our School Press.

CUDWORTH
SENIOR BOYS' SCHOOL
FANCIERS' CLUB

FIRST PRIZE

AWARDED TO _____

FOR _____

Cudworth Secondary Modern schoolboys after completing their swimming proficiency tests September 1935.

The successful Secondary Modern boys football team after winning the Felkirk Trophy in the school's first year of operation in April 1936.

COUNTY COUNCIL OF THE WEST RIDING OF YORKSHIRE

CUDWORTH

COUNTY SECONDARY SCHOOL

OPENING OF THE SCHOOL
SPEECH DAY
PRIZE GIVING

2nd July, 1968

Cudworth Secondary Modern became a County Secondary school in the early 1950s and the educational division of boys and girls finished soon after. Here is the program for the speech day and prize giving in July 1968.

CUDWORTH COUNTY SECONDARY SCHOOL STAFF

Mrs. M. Oxley	Headmistress
Mr. D. J. Curry	Deputy Headmaster
Miss J. Goodall	Senior Mistress
Mr. D. H. Barker	Head of Lower School & Rural Studies
Mr. D. L. Hoddle	Head of Upper School & English
Mr. A. A. Smith	Head of Handicraft (Boys)
Mrs. M. Wigglesworth	Head of Handicraft (Girls)
Mr. N. Buckley	Head of Maths
Mr. V. Hemingway	Librarian & History
Mrs. M. Hanstock	Senior Teacher of Domestic Science
Mr. G. R. Turton	Careers Master & Metalwork
Mr. I. A. Atkinson	Senior Science Teacher
Mrs. C. Dutton	Senior Art Teacher
Mr. P. Horbury	Senior Geography Teacher
Mr. R. J. Bone	Outdoor Pursuits Organiser, Art & Geography
Mr. K. Nield	Senior Master Boys' Physical Education
Mr. C. D. Healey	Head of Music
Mrs. S. Jenkinson	History & Music
Mrs. E. Paling	Domestic Science
Mr. K. Newton	Geography & Library
Mrs. V. Kay	Physical Education
Mrs. C. Horbury	Biology & Chemistry
Mr. P. Kaye	English & Drama
Miss E. Green	History & Religious Knowledge
Miss E. Jacobs	Maths & Science
Miss S. Cawthorn	English & Drama
Mr. D. Want	Peripatetic Brass Teacher

The staff in attendance for the speech day in 1968.

A Secondary school three week working holiday in Italy in 1970 included visits to Naples, Rome and Sorrento. Those identified so far are: Dave Ewett, David Marshall, Julie Harrison, Mary Oxley (headteacher), Dave Tye, David Wilmot, Nigel Archer, John Fenn, Dave Shaw.

Cudworth County Secondary girls pose before setting off for Holland in 1961.

Winners of the girls sports day trophies for 1957. They are, left to right: Ruth Auckland, Carol Legate, Kathleen Worrall, Pauline Shepherd, Carol Thorpe.

Susan Shaw receives the house sports trophy from headmistress Mary Oxley at the baths in 1962.

Cudworth Secondary Girls netball team winners of the Felkirk Trophy in 1957.

Cudworth Secondary Girls rounders team winners of the Hemsworth and District Rounders League in 1955.

House cup winners June 1954. Left to right: D. White, A. Dable, V. Ramsbottom, B. Ball, L. Larkin.

School prefects of 1961. Back row, left to right: Marguerite Perks, Margaret Cole, Mary Hewitt, Shelia Williams, Barbara Pearson. Front row: Pamela Victory, Dorothy Goose, Mrs Oxley (headmistress), Carol Peaker, Susan Shaw.

Girls of Cudworth Secondary school performed the English adaptation of the classic Chinese play *Lady Precious Stream* by H.S. Hsuing in March 1958. This particular play lasts for over six hours but had been considerably trimmed for the three nights it played at the school hall. The lead role (Precious Stream) was taken by eleven-year-old Emma Wright and described by the *Barnsley Chronicle* as a performance of great 'delicacy and charm'.

CUDWORTH GIRLS' SCHOOL

presents

" Lady Precious Stream "

by S. I. HSIUNG

For **THREE NIGHTS**

TUESDAY, WEDNESDAY and THURSDAY
MARCH 25th, 26th and 27th, 1958

in the SCHOOL HALL at 6-45 p.m.

ADMISSION 2/-

Row No............ Seat No............ Day..

Snydale Junior team – winners of the Felkirk Cup in 1948.

In 'the yard' at Snydale 1950.

Snydale Juniors on a school camp in Suffolk in 1950.

Cudworth Secondary Modern junior cross-country team 1960-61 – Barnsley and District Champions.

Sage advice from the Mayor to girls from Cudworth Secondary as they prepare for their swimming certificates at the open air pool, c. 1955.

Eight

Sport and Leisure Times

Cudworth Operatic Society performed *Pirates of Penzance* to packed audiences in 1943. Those identified so far are Harold Wright, Ruby Warsop, Headley Morgan (musical director).

The West End Choir in the 1940s. Those identified are Harold Gascoigne, Norman Rigby, Cliff Schoral, Harold Wright, Ronnie Rigby, Edward Attlee, Ken Wallace.

Ernest Blenkinsop, one of Cudworth's most famous sons and gifted full-back, in 1924. Ernie was brought up in Churchfield Avenue (just off Church Street) and played football for school and village before being signed by Hull City. He went on to play for Sheffield Wednesday, Liverpool, and Cardiff City as well as captaining England.

Cudworth Village Football Club 1921-22.

Cudworth Village Football Club 1937-38.

Dorothy Hyman – superb athlete and Cudworth born and bred. She was brought up at Blomfontein Street, just off the Barnsley Road; her father worked at Monk Bretton colliery and Dorothy attended the junior school and from 1952 Cudworth Secondary Modern. In an old, carefully preserved scrapbook kept at the Barnsley Archive Service, a proud teacher has listed Dorothy's achievements over the years: from winning the hop, skip and jump in 1953 to her Olympic performances. Her destiny seemed to be set when she wrote these prophetic words in a school essay: 'When I grow up to be a lady I would like to be a great runner... perhaps an Olympic champion' (Dorothy Hyman – *Sprint to Fame*, 1964). She became a member of the Hickleton Main Club and trained on the club fields near Thurnscoe. Other famous members of this club included the boxers Billy Thompson and Ron 'Tubby' Latham (see *Goldthorpe, Thurnscoe and Bolton-upon-Dearne* edition) – not a bad pedigree for small colliery welfare organisation. Dorothy won the 100 and 150 yards at the Barnsley Schools championships in 1956 and in that year also became Yorkshire County champion and All-England Schools winner at 100 yards.

'Old' former student Dorothy Hyman presents trophies to pupils from the school in the early 1960s. Arguments will always abound over 'who was the greatest' but Cudworth's favourite daughter must rank as one of the greatest British sportswomen (perhaps only surpassed by the achievements of her contemporary Mary Rand). When she was only seventeen she won a gold medal when she ran the second leg for the British 110 yds relay team in the Empire Games at Cardiff; in 1960 at the Rome Olympics she took silver in the 100 m (11.3 seconds) and bronze in the 200 m (24.7 seconds); in the Belgrade European Championships of 1962 she took gold in the 100 m (11.3 seconds) and silver in the 200 m (23.7 seconds) – a performance she repeated at Perth Empire Games in the same year. In 1963 she broke a former male preserve and won the BBC's Sports Personality of the Year. Despite all her fame Dorothy remained a very down to earth Yorkshire lass as much of her autobiography demonstrates: 'It's an ordinary place is Cudworth: a pit village four miles out of Barnsley on the Pontefract road where most of us talk with the same south Yorkshire accents. We don't say 'the village' but 't'village – we speak not of 'coming home' but of 'coomin hawm' ... men love to stick to their old cloth caps and women are apt to walk about the streets with their hair in curlers' (*Sprint to Fame* 1964). The Dorothy Hyman track on the Snydale Road was built in honour of her achievements and, remaining true to her roots, she still lives in the Barnsley area.

Local speedway rider Bert Round, pictured here in 1929, won numerous trophies throughout the South Yorkshire area. Such were his talents that he was soon signed to ride for one of the biggest teams in the north – the Sheffield Tigers. He won the 'Golden Helmet' at the Hillsborough stadium so many times that when he was tragically killed in an off-track motorcycling accident, the Sheffield promoters renamed the helmet the Bert Round Golden Helmet Memorial Trophy.

The Cudworth village cricket team from 1959.

Cudworth railway cricket team in the 1930s: the team consisted of station and engineering workers from the Cudworth line. Sitting in the centre of the group is Jack Simons.

The Cudworth cricket club ('A' team) in 1946.

Shafton school junior cricket team in 1950. The junior school was then known locally as Shafton 'Two Gates' Council school. Pictured here are back row, left to right: Reg Giles, Terry Jolley, John Hotchen, Mr Kenneth Lawton, Terry Lee, Lewis Kelsall, Frank Lightfoot. Middle row: Malcolm Josham, Peter Glew, Brian Moore, Ken Bramham, Geoff Govier. Front row: Colin Archer, Hugh Livett.

Shafton school junior cricket team in 1949. Back row, left to right: Reg Giles, Lewis Kelsall, John Hotchen, Albert Day, Mr Kenneth Lawson, Henry Vamplew, Brian Goose, Malcolm Josham. Middle row: Frank Lightfoot, Douglas Boyden, Brain Moore, Jack Schofield, Michael Cooke, Geoff Govier, Michael Buckingham. Front row: Don Milton, Tommy Kelsall.

Shafton school football team 1948. Back row, left to right: Peter Glew, John Hotchen, Malcolm Josham, Mr Kenneth Lawton, Terry Lee, Tommy Bailey. Middle row: Colin Archer, Terry Jolley, Brian Moore, Frank Lightfoot, Geoff Govier. Front: Reg Giles, Hugh Livett. (These pictures of the Shafton teams have been reproduced with the kind permission of Mr Geoff Govier).

Grimethorpe Football team in 1920.

A large group of 'regulars' stand outside their local the Star Inn on the Barnsley Road, *c.* 1905 and judging by the numbers the pub was as extremely popular at the turn of the century as it is today. This particular building was replaced with the present inn during the 1920s; the present landlord is Robert Sykes.

Cudworth and Grimethorpe Home Guard 1940. This group formed the 'A' Company Signal section; the only member identified so far is Mr Charles 'Charlie' Beaumont.

The whole of 'A' Company Home Guard at Cudworth in the 1940s.

Nine

Shops and Businesses

Globe Tea Company staff outside the shop on the Crescent at Cudworth in 1910 which is today the site of the Anchor Press. The Globe Tea Company was a national chain of tea 'shops' that sold a range of blended leaves in the days before the invention of the tea bag.

The Co-op (No. 39) on the Pontefract Road at Cudworth in 1910. The Barnsley Co-operative Society began in humble premises in Market Street in 1862 but by the turn of the century it had numerous branches throughout the area. Today, especially for a younger generation weaned upon the indoor shopping complex and large retail parks, it is difficult to imagine the integral part the Co-op played in the lives of ordinary folk. Every local person had a membership number. The 'divi' [dividend] was given out twice yearly and school children even received classes in how and why the Co-operative Society had been founded. Most Co-ops at this time presented few luxuries and concentrated on selling the essentials of life – tea, butter, cheese, soap etc.

Bagg's boot and shoe shop on the Barnsley Road in 1903.

Mr Mosley's grocery shop in the 1920s was situated at 243 Barnsley Road in Cudworth.

A 'sweet' shop on the Barnsley Road at the turn of the twentieth century – the name of the owners of this particular shop remains unresolved.

Above: Turner's farm shop in Cudworth, *c.* 1930.

Left: Cudworth bootmaking. This picture is possibly of Edwin Brunt, bootmaker, who operated from 334 Barnsley Road. In 1908 three other bootmakers are listed as operating businesses: Joshua Davis (1, St John's Road), Edward Milner (Barnsley Road), John Grice (77, St John's Road).

Staff outside Newton's garage on the Pontefract Road, *c.* 1930.

Pratt's Garage, Pontefract Road, *c.* 1930.

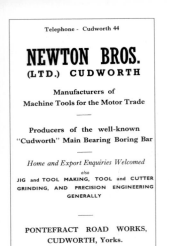

Telephone - Cudworth 44

NEWTON BROS.
(LTD.) CUDWORTH

Manufacturers of
Machine Tools for the Motor Trade

———

Producers of the well-known
"Cudworth" Main Bearing Boring Bar

———

Home and Export Enquiries Welcomed
also
JIG and TOOL MAKING, TOOL and CUTTER
GRINDING, AND PRECISION ENGINEERING
GENERALLY

———

PONTEFRACT ROAD WORKS,
CUDWORTH, Yorks.

6

WOODCOCK'S GARAGE

(Proprietor : W. A. WOODCOCK),

SCHOOL HILL,
CUDWORTH,

TELEPHONE 40.   NEAR BARNSLEY.

Automobile & Mechanical Engineers.

| ACCUMULATOR AND WIRELESS SERVICE STATION. | OXY-ACETYLENE WELDING AND MACHINE WORK. |

All kinds of Electrical Equipment supplied.

Left: An advertisement for Newton Brothers in 1940. Note the telephone number – Cudworth 44. Right: A Woodcock's garage advert c. 1928.

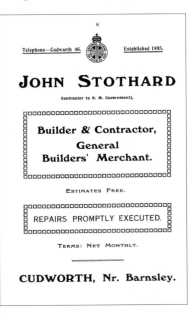

8

Telephone—Cudworth 46.   Established 1895.

JOHN STOTHARD

Contractor to H. M. Government),

Builder & Contractor,
General
Builders' Merchant.

ESTIMATES FREE.

REPAIRS PROMPTLY EXECUTED.

TERMS: NET MONTHLY.

CUDWORTH, Nr. Barnsley.

CUDWORTH HEALTH WEEK, 1928.

Healthy Homes.

CLEANLINESS in the home should be one of the maxims of everyone's life. Paint and Papers are cheap, and there is no surer way of attaining and keeping a healthy state in your home, than by regular interior decoration. We shall be glad, at any time, to give you our advice as to how this may be most economically done.

Office & Shop Work a Speciality.

Contractors for Exterior Decorations.

WALLPAPERS.   LEATHERETTES.

PAINTS.   VARNISHES.

DISTEMPERS, Etc.

Agents for Aslin Paper Blinds.

TELPHONE—CUDWORTH 35.

PEMBERTON & BUTCHER,

Painters and Decorators,

212, BARNSLEY ROAD, CUDWORTH,

and at Pontefract Road.

USE GAS

FOR

LIGHTING, HEATING

AND

COOKING.

GAS is the silent SERVANT and friend of the house-wife, its WAGES are LOW and need only be paid by instalments of ONE PENNY EACH.

CUT OUT

DUST, DIRT AND DRUDGERY,

and thereby improve your HEALTH by using a GAS Cooker, GAS Heated Wash Copper, GAS Fire, or a GAS Iron.

Prompt attention will be given to any enquiries received at the GAS WORKS, or the Council Offices,

CUDWORTH

URBAN DISTRICT COUNCIL

GAS DEPARTMENT.

Cudworth Gas Department (part of the Urban District Council) offering gas installation for 1d!

Ten

Celebrations, Processions and Worship

A group outside St. John the Baptist church Cudworth in 1962. Back rows: Ken Bryant, Billy Osbourne, David Mosley, -?-, -?-, Ernest Blenkinsop, Sidney Jackson, Bernard McGrath, Christopher Brumpton, Brain Chappel, Desmond Currie, John Burton, ? Benstead, Willie Dodd, Eric Thornton, Norman Higgs, Harold Chappel. Front: -?-, Father Brumpton, David Hubbard, Dave Shaw.

A church nativity play at Cudworth St. George's Hall in 1958. Those pictured are Veronica Brumpton, Susan Shaw, Katherine Wincupp, Janet Midgeley, Dorothy Shotbolt, Ruth Davies, Denise Davies, Linda Rigby, Linda Hatton, Andrea Burton, June Wilkinson, Jennifer Hinchcliffe.

The church queen sits with her subjects at The Pond in 1958. They are Susan Shaw, Janet Midgeley, Ruth Davies, Denise Davies, Veronica Brumpton, Andrea Burton, Susan Burton.

Cudworth church, c. 1910. The parish church was built in 1893 by public subscription at a cost of £2,592 with a seating capacity for 350 people.

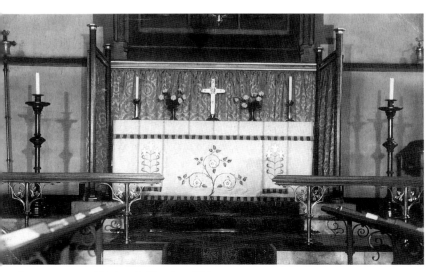

An interior view of Cudworth Church, c. 1910.

Outside Cudworth church in 1920.

A harvest celebration inside Cudworth church in 1905.

Cudworth Methodist New Connexion Band of Hope in 1905. Note the beautifully decorated crosses which must have taken hours to produce.

Exquisite decorations inside the chapel at Cudworth 1905.

The church and vicarage in 1920. The vicarage is now the site of an Old People's home.

The vicarage not long after its construction. Note the newly planted lawn and flower beds.

Cudworth brass band outside the John Smith Memorial chapel on Barnsley Road, c. 1905. The chapel is named after the Rev. John Smith and opened in June 1892. Behind the chapel stands the sunday school which is presently used as a Youth Club run by enthusistic locals for the benefit of all. Recent suggestions have included pulling down the school and offering the land for sale; hopefully provision will be made for the younger members of the community if such a sale proceeds.

A New Connexion chapel parade past the Crescent and through The Pond in 1905.

A Union Jack is hoisted aloft by First Class Petty Officer Longley during Coronation celebrations at the Crescent on 22 June 1911. After ten years of rule Edward VIII had died to be succeeded by his brother George but this was a period of great uncertainty for the country. Over nearly one hundred Britain had prospered under Victoria and later Edward but the death of the monarch seemed to bring a loss of security: world economic supremacy was being surpassed by Germany and the United States; the suffragette movement had turned to militancy to win women the vote while the prospect of war grew closer as crisis followed crisis in Europe.

Right: The Coronation bonfire at Cudworth in 1911. The bonfire and a large firework display were the evening highlights of a day of celebration. After the raising of the flag a procession went down the Barnsley Road, Manor Road, Lunn Road, Whitecross Road to the Snydale Road School. The firework display took place at Kiln Croft just behind the old Star Hotel; the bonfire was on the official list for the King's Coronation and consisted of 20 tons of timber (mostly old railway sleepers), a barrel of tar, and was 30 feet high and 14 feet in diameter.

Below: A Shafton and District Band of Hope demonstration proceeds along the Pontefract Road in 1906.

The Cudworth queen (and her entourage) travel in a regal style on the back of a truck past Fentons on the Barnsley Road, *c.* 1953.

The Cudworth Amalgamated Society of Railway Servants orphan fund procession on the Barnsley Road in 1909. This particular picture was probably taken from one of the windows at the Star Inn.

The Amalgamated Society of Railway Servants orphan procession reaches the edge of Cudworth on the Barnsley Road in 1909. Note the beautifully crafted A.S.R.S banner being held aloft.

The A.S.R.S. procession 1909.

Kids in fancy dress formed part of the celebrations at Shafton for the Coronation of Elizabeth II in 1953. This dray was later pulled around the streets with cheering children 'draped' around the sides.

Most of the work during the day was done by two appropriately decorated Shire horses – used to pull groups of Shafton children around the village. In the background is the Shafton junior school which became the focal point for celebrations.

Fancy dress was *de rigeur* for all local children; costumes including red indians, cowboys and a variety of pirates. Pictured second from the left here is Jenine Baker.

Eleven

Transport and Industry

A National Coal Board sign marks the boundary of the Grimethorpe Colliery – a picture taken shortly before the colliery closed in 1993. The Grimethorpe sinkings began on 8 October 1894 and were cut by Mr G.H. Turner of the Midland Railway (his efforts were described by the *Barnsley Chronicle*, somewhat tongue-in-cheek, as 'workmanlike'). There were two original shafts and the first estimates put a possible extraction of over 2,500 tons a day. In 1896 the original owners of the colliery, Mitchell Main Collieries, were bought out by Yorkshire and Derbyshire Coal and Iron Company (they also owned Carlton Main) and as the shafts reached the Barnsley seam full production began in earnest.

A long line of wagons stands idle in the yard after the closure of the pit. In May 1993 the last 210 working men at the pit elected by a vote of two to one to accept British Coal's offer of redundancy. It was yet another blow to area's economic and social fortunes; as Ken Hancock, the N.U.M. branch secretary said at the time: 'There seems to be a cloud of despair hanging over the whole community' (*Barnsley Chronicle*, 7 May 1993).

A view over the colliery in 1993.

Two of the old winding wheels stand idle at the colliery. With a desperate irony it was announced that in the last six months before closure the colliery had actually made a profit of well over one million pounds; but as Chris Cotton, Grimethorpe N.U.M. delegate, stated 'by now neither British Coal or the Government seem to care'.

In the early hours of Thursday 19 January 1905 three express trains were involved in a collision which killed six people and seriously injured over twenty.

CUDWORTH RAILWAY ACCIDENT, 19/1/05

The scene of the accident was a stretch of line at Storrs Mill between Dartfield and Cudworth.

A mail train from Leeds destined for Sheffield passed a junction in heavy mist in the early hours. A fish truck, which had been connected to the rear of the train, became derailed and pulled over several coaches which remained across the tracks. Travelling behind was the Scotch Express from Glasgow destined for St Pancras which ploughed into the wreakage of the mail train at speed of over sixty miles per hour. The lead engine on the Scotch Express and many of the front coaches crashed down an embankment; escaping gas then ignited causing the wreakage to burn fiercely. The fire attracted colliery workers at Grimethorpe who rushed over the fields to help the injured. As the flames took hold further catastrophe was narrowly avoided as another Express, travelling from St Pancras to Scotland, managed to pull-up only yards from the scene after the driver had noticed the frantic waves of a local goods guard.

The aftermath of the crash: debris and wreakage was spread over several hundred yards of track including several thousand parcels and letters from Scotland and the North-East destined for the Midlands. As the local paper reported the scene was somewhat macrabre: 'Larger numbers of people were at the scene of the disaster quite early, and throughout the day there were large numbers of curious spectators, who beheld such a sight as probably few, if any of them, had ever witnessed before' (*Barnsley Chronicle*, 21 January 1905).

SCOTCH EXPRESS COLLISION CUDWORTH Jany 19 1905 Barnsley Photo Co

MIDLAND RAILWAY STATION, CUDWORTH.

A view overlooking Cudworth station in 1905. It is very difficult to envisage where the station at Cudworth stood – only a few remnants are visible. However, if you stand near the tracks at the back of the Newlands Estate and overlooking Lundwood it is possible to imagine the scene at the turn of the century with the platforms packed with people travelling to points all over the country. Local people would walk to the station over land which is today the site of the Newlands estate and pick up 'a push and pull' service for Barnsley. The main line linking Derby and Leeds, built in 1840, stopped at Cudworth – chosen to act as the main station for Barnsley. A connecting line into town was added in 1870 with a further extension to Wombwell in 1899.

Railway staff at Cudworth station in 1920.

Above: A view over the locomotive sheds at Cudworth 1947.

Left: An old and defunct signal box at Cudworth south junction 1979. Only a single line on the track remains open today – used for industrial wagons.

Miners receiving strike pay at Cudworth during the General Strike of 1926. The threat of a General Strike had been looming over the country, provoked by a crisis in the mining industry. A foolhardy return to the old gold standard in 1925 had forced exporters throughout Britain to raise their prices abroad with a consequent fall in orders. The coal industry was among the worst hit and in June 1925 the owners (the industry at that time was still a private concern) responded by reducing wages and lengthening working hours. The miners rallied under the famous cry of 'Not a penny off the pay, not a minute on the day'. A temporary reprieve was bought by the undertaking of a Royal Commission headed by Sir Herbert Samuel but in May 1926 the miners were locked out of the collieries. The Trades Union Congress called for a nation-wide stoppage and for the next nine days industry ground to a halt. However, the government under Stanley Baldwin called upon the armed forces and thousands of volunteers to keep the country going and on 12 May the T.U.C. called off the strike. The miners felt betrayed by the decision and remained on strike for a further six months – only starvation forcing them back to the pits. For many in the country the strike had been an extended holiday – the chance for students to drive buses and trains – but for the miners in South Yorkshire it was a painful hiatus of hunger and poverty.

Workers take a break to pose for the camera, c. 1920. In the background are the nearly completed homes on the Snydale estate – one of a series of council housing plans to cater for the growing Cudworth population.

Newsagents
Tobacconists
Confectioners

ESTABLISHED OVER A
QUARTER OF A CENTURY

*Fairly extensive area
covered for news delivery*

*Good choice of sweets
and chocolates*

*Very good range of
cigarettes*

H. & C. M. SCHORAH

218 BARNSLEY ROAD
Telephone 418 Cudworth

A series of adverts for Cudworth shops and businsses in 1950 – many will be familiar to local people.

*Plumbers and
Heating Engineers*

Montague House

Pontefract Road

Cudworth

Telephone 401

GAS, SOLID FUEL, OIL
small bore and warm
air duct

**NCB Housewarming
plan**

**Bathroom
conversions and
extensions**

COMPREHENSIVE RANGE OF
PATTERNED GLASS
STOCKED

S. DRIVER
and SON